WINE
PLACES

PHOTOGRAPHS BY CHARLES O'REAR

WORDS BY DAVID FURER

WINE PLACES

the land, the wine, the people

Wine Places
Photographs by Charles O'Rear
Words by David Furer

First published in Great Britain in 2005 by Mitchell Beazley,
an imprint of Octopus Publishing Group Ltd,
2–4 Heron Quays, London E14 4JP

Copyright © Octopus Publishing Group Ltd 2005
Photographs copyright © Charles O'Rear, St Helena, California
and Corbis Corporation, Seattle, Washington, USA

ISBN 1 84533 112 5

A CIP record for this book is available from the British Library

Set in Sabon, Engravers

Printed and bound in China by Toppan Printing
Company Limited

Commissioning Editor   Hilary Lumsden
Executive Art Editor   Yasia Williams
Managing Editor   Juanne Branquinho
Editor   Susanna Forbes
Design   Colin Goody
Production   Jane Rogers

The publishers will be grateful for any information that will
assist them in keeping future editions up-to-date. Although all
reasonable care has been taken in the preparation of this book,
neither the publishers nor the author can accept any liability
for any consequence arising from the use thereof, or the
information contained therein.

Charles O'Rear can be contacted at charles@wineviews.com

CONTENTS

PREFACE

As you leaf through this book, imagine you are on a journey to the world's wine producing regions. Find yourself on a cold, damp winter morning in the Médoc region of Bordeaux. Notice the smells. Feel the crisp temperatures. Now you're walking through a hot February vineyard in Chile's Maipo valley and listening to the workers sing. Enter an underground cellar in California and taste ageing wine from the barrel. Realize that these experiences – smells, sounds and tastes – can't be conveyed in photographs, but images can, and that's why this book is in your hands.

Photographs are about visuals and, fortunately, wine regions around the world display striking backdrops and colourful beauty. Add the often dramatic architecture of wineries and the symmetry of vineyards with these beautiful wine places and your senses are further heightened. A bunch of grapes and a bottle of wine may look the same everywhere in the world, but all the work in between becomes fair game for a camera.

Agriculture and rural living have been familiar to me since childhood – I grew up in America's heartland surrounded by cornfields. Therefore, it was no surprise when I found myself attracted to grape-growing regions and, of course, the wines they produce. My passion grew when I was sent to California's Napa Valley in 1978 to photograph an article for *National Geographic* magazine. I moved to the valley while continuing to photograph around the world for the magazine. My assignments took me to subjects ranging from technology to archaeology, while along the way I also encountered the wheat-cutters of Ukraine, the rice-harvesters of Asia, and the coconut growers of the Tropics. But the art of growing wine grapes continued to stir my emotions and to excite my creativity. When I found myself pursuing grape harvests around the world, I soon discovered that winter never comes to the earth's wine regions. Every season of the year, wine grapes are in harvest somewhere between 30° and 50° latitude north and south of the equator. These temperate zones combined with the right soils produce ideal conditions for *Vitis vinifera*, the grapevine species most used for wine grapes.

So, here is my vision of wine places around the world. With this book, I invite you to come with me while I take you flying over vineyards, inside the wineries, and deep underground into their cellars. Along the way, you will feel the fun of stomping grapes for homemade wine, view the giant châteaux of France, look over a foggy Napa Valley sunrise from Spring Mountain, experience workers descending steep vineyards along the Rhône, walk with me into a Portuguese forest to watch cork bark being removed from trees and, finally, watch the pressing of Syrah at a family-run Australian winery.

There is an expression that photographs can be worth a thousand words, but words add important information and offer a context and background that is not always available through the camera alone. Writer, wine educator, and Advanced Sommelier David Furer shares my passions about the world of wine. Through his accompanying text, he brings a valuable dimension to this book that I am sure will be appreciated by readers everywhere.

As you journey through these pages, I hope that you will enjoy the land, the wine, and the people, for it is all of these components that somehow miraculously come together to create a sensual and visual experience like nothing on earth.

Charles O'Rear, St. Helena, California

LEFT AUTUMN BRINGS A RUSTIC
PALETTE OF COLOURS TO CALISTOGA
IN THE NORTH OF THE NAPA VALLEY

BELOW GOLDEN HUES ALSO
DOMINATE THIS ANTINORI VINEYARD IN
THE TUSCAN VILLAGE OF PASSIGNANO

IT ALL BEGINS IN THE VINEYARDS, THE SOURCE OF THE FRUIT THAT PRODUCES WINE, THE BEVERAGE BRINGING US TO THESE PAGES. WITH OUR PLANET'S COMPLEX GEOLOGICAL HISTORY, LAND AND WATER FORMATIONS ACROSS THE GLOBE TAKE THEIR DEVELOPMENT FROM VARIOUS TIME PERIODS. SOMETIMES THESE PIECES OF LAND ARE AS SMALL AS AN ISOLATED OUTCROP OR AS LARGE AS AN ENTIRE PLAIN. ONE WAY IN WHICH THE OLD AND NEW WORLDS OF WINE ARE OFTEN DISTINGUISHED IS IN THE MANNER IN WHICH VINEYARDS HAVE BEEN SELECTED. WHEREAS THE OLD WORLD HAS HAD CENTURIES TO LET THE BEST MATCH BETWEEN SITE AND VARIETY FIND ITSELF, GRAPE-GROWING IN THE NEW WORLD IS RATHER MORE RECENT, AND THUS LESS INFLUENCED BY THE HISTORICAL MACHINATIONS OF CHURCH AND SECULAR RULERS.

REFLECTIONS OF THE VINE

locations, landscapes, and vineyards

Vineyards in the New World continue to be chosen for their suitability for viticulture, to be sure, but also for their proximity to the population centres of their respective countries. These towns are located mainly on flatter and/or more easily traversed land than their Old World counterparts, and the vineyards – along with other food sources – tend to be near the town too.

In the early days, security from strange beasts and potentially hostile natives was a primary concern. The vineyards tended to be at the same elevation as the villages and were selected more for their fertility than anything else. Climates tended to be warmer than those in most of Europe, and the vineyards were not necessarily well-suited to the finer wine grape varieties.

Such mismatches were not always the case, the most striking testament to this being a 1976 blind tasting in Paris. Noted wine critic Stephen Spurrier, in those days a wine merchant, pitted the best of France and California against each other. The assembled tasters, mostly French, chose Stag's Leap Wine Cellars Cabernet Sauvignon over all other reds, beating some of Bordeaux's top châteaux.

PREVIOUS PAGE THE CYCLE BEGINS AGAIN AS BUDS BEGIN TO BURST, SEEN HERE IN A DUNDEE HILLS VINEYARD IN WILLAMETTE VALLEY, OREGON

BELOW HISTORY MEETS HORTICULTURE IN THE BURGUNDIAN VILLAGE OF FUISSE, WHERE VINES SNUGGLE UP TO THE LOCAL CHURCH

BELOW RIGHT VINE TENDRILS REACH FOR THE SKY AT BARNETT VINEYARDS IN THE NAPA VALLEY

TOP RIGHT CABERNET IS KING IN PRIME SITES SUCH AS THOSE OF NAPA'S FAMED STAG'S LEAP WINE CELLARS

Technology and its ability to enable humans to move mountains changed the nature of how a vineyard can be chosen. In the late twentieth century, wine-growers had the option of either planting the fields as they were, or sculpting the land into shapes that better suited their idea of how best use could be made of the land available.

This was not necessarily a new notion. The ancient Romans built terraces along the banks of the Rhône River valley, then along Germany's Mosel River valley. And the terraced vineyards of the home of port, the windswept, sun-baked Douro River valley of northern Portugal, saw their birth in the seventeenth century. With dense schistous soils, these terraces are the only way for the vine to cling onto the often steep slopes. But the labour required to maintain these historic walls is great, hence numerous trials have taken place in an effort to find a less costly way of securing the vines' safety.

Germany developed more modern methods with its *Flurbereinigung* or vineyard remodelling, which reached its heyday in the 1970s. Although it met with some resistance, including claims that it would alter the

PREVIOUS PAGE MORNING SKIES GREET A NET-COVERED VINEYARD AT HAWKE'S BAY, NEW ZEALAND, WHERE BIRDS ARE ONE OF THE KEY THREATS

TOP LEFT MODERN METHODS SUCH AS LYRE TRELLISSING, POPULAR IN CALIFORNIA, PROVIDE THE BEST CONDITIONS FOR THE VINE TO THRIVE

BELOW LEFT THE GENTLE SLOPES OF THE COLDSTREAM HILLS VINEYARD NEAR MELBOURNE, AUSTRALIA

BELOW PROUD OF HIS GERMANIC ORIGINS, THE CALIFORNIAN PIONEER FREDERICK BERINGER BUILT HIS RHINE HOUSE IN ST HELENA IN 1883

character of the wines – and in many cases it did – the voices of the growers won the day. Other European countries such as Luxembourg adopted this policy too.

Most Old World wine-growing regions have evolved in a more "organic" fashion than their New World counterparts, emerging through a process primarily dictated by historical and economic imperative. Many vineyards here rest upon soils relatively infertile for crops more critical for human survival, notably grains, or at a degree too steep for easy retention of water. These lands were first farmed by unlucky peasants considered, in the eyes of the local noble, unworthy to possess a bit of more fertile "bottom land". If they eked out an existence on the poor soils they were granted, it was not for long. Eventually, when the peasant died or had to find other means of support, these parcels would revert to the reigning noble.

Does the land shape the temperament of its people? If one looks at what are arguably the two greatest wine districts in Germany, one might say "yes". The Mosel River valley is so steep that it is commonly said that its

PREVIOUS PAGE LEFT VITAL TO ANY VINE'S SUCCESS, WATER REMAINS A KEY THEME IN THE PLANNING OF ANY VINEYARD

PREVIOUS PAGE RIGHT A PERFECT CABERNET LEAF SOAKS UP THE MEDOC SUN AT BORDEAUX WINERY, COS D'ESTOURNEL

LEFT STEEP SLOPES LIKE THOSE OF EGON MULLER IN THE SAAR REGION OF GERMANY ARE ONE OF THE FACTORS BEHIND RIESLING'S SUCCESS

ABOVE AS THE MORNING FOG LIFTS, DELICATE BEADS OF MOISTURE FORM ON TRELLIS WIRE AT COS D'ESTOURNEL

inhabitants have one leg shorter than the other. The river curls through the land like a snake, with vineyards broken up into many small parcels. A little guarded today, in the more poverty-stricken times of the mid-nineteenth century the Mosellers were considered a touch envious of their neighbours. Just as nature provided barriers making it difficult to see the activities of neighbours, so it afforded the Mosellers a degree of privacy. By comparison the Rheingau, although steep in parts, is by no means as foreboding and difficult to work as the Mosel, and its vineyards are grouped into larger parcels. Just as one can easily see what one's neighbour is up to, so the character of the people also seems more open and accessible.

The serpentine nature of the Douro River valley might lead one to think that its people have a similar approach to life as the inhabitants of the Mosel. Conspiring against this conclusion is the remoteness of the valley's interior, limiting what can be done alone and thus engendering more of a team spirit. Another factor might be the abundance of sun and its effect upon the disposition of the locals.

PREVIOUS PAGE THE STUNNING LAKE WANAKA HELPS TO MODERATE THE CLIMATE OF RIPPON VINEYARDS ON THE SOUTH ISLAND OF NEW ZEALAND

LEFT FROM AGE COMES BEAUTY, BOTH TO THE EYE AND TO THE GLASS, SINCE OLD VINES SUCH AS THIS ONE FROM COONAWARRA IN AUSTRALIA TEND TO PRODUCE WINES OF GREATER CHARACTER AND INTENSITY

BELOW STANDING TO ATTENTION, A REGIMENT OF NAPA VALLEY VINES SPORT THEIR AUTUMNAL COLOURS

The grape vine's popularity rose in the Middle Ages since it was widely considered to be the source of a healthy drink. Unless provided by a well or a spring, fresh water was seen as the potential bearer of a wealth of maladies. Louis Pasteur, a native of Jura in France, hadn't yet been born to discover the action of yeasts and alcohol. However, from a historically drawn-out and pleasant method of trial and error, people discovered that the grape not only provided energy and liquid in a variety of tastes and colours, it didn't make its consumers quite so ill as water, at least when consumed in moderation.

As we have seen, the decision of where to locate a vineyard remains a complex one. Factors to consider include: topography, the position and elevation of the land; aspect, how it relates to the sun's position; climate, defined as the general meteorological conditions of temperature, rain, and wind; and weather, the conditions at a specific time and place in relation to variables such as temperature, sun, wind velocity, and barometric pressure. Soil content and its porosity – does it drain well, for example – make a significant difference to the overall

PREVIOUS PAGE TREE-COVERED HILLTOPS SHELTER SOUGHT-AFTER CABERNET AND MERLOT VINES IN NAPA VALLEY'S DIAMOND MOUNTAIN

BELOW SUNRISE BACKLIGHTS A CABERNET VINE LEAF AT NEWTON VINEYARDS, ST HELENA, CALIFORNIA

RIGHT RICH RED SOIL DOMINATES THE HUNTER VALLEY LANDSCAPE, NORTH OF SYDNEY

quality of a particular vineyard and help to determine the grape variety planted. Economic considerations play their part, as does proximity to fresh water for irrigation, and roads for transport. In many countries, there are legal restrictions on what areas and what varietals can be planted that have to be taken into account. Finally, consumer demand, by no means a new idea, has become more of a planned-for concern the world over during the wine "boom" of the past few decades.

Although some of the world's most praised wines emanate from locations that are relatively unremarkable in their appearance – take sherry and Bordeaux, for instance – there are great panoramic vistas in countless other wine-growing spots. Think of Burgundy's Hill of Corton and the surrounding vineyards within the Clos du Vougeot. Or Rhône's Swiss Valais vineyards, with the Hill of Hermitage downstream and the amphitheatre of Château Grillet in between. Or Piedmont's cloud-shrouded Barolo hills, Germany's strikingly-steep Mosel vineyards, and the Cape Town wineries in the awesome shadow of Table Mountain – and that's just for starters.

PREVIOUS PAGE THE COOLING EFFECT OF MORNING FOG RISING THROUGH THE PINES OF NAPA'S SPRING MOUNTAIN LEADS TO FINER GRAPES

LEFT TRADITIONAL TECHNIQUES SUCH AS THE USE OF CANES TO TIE VINES STILL HAVE THEIR PLACE, AS SEEN HERE IN THIS VALPOLICELLA VINEYARD NEAR MARONA, NORTH OF VERONA

ABOVE NETS ARE USED TO KEEP HUNGRY BIRDS OFF JUICY CHARDONNAY GRAPES IN THE YARRA VALLEY, AUSTRALIA

LEFT PLENTY OF SUN AND ENOUGH
RAIN MEANS A GOOD HARVEST FOR
CABERNET IN THE NAPA VALLEY

BELOW AN ARMY OF PICKERS REPORT
FOR DUTY IN THE VINEYARDS OF
CALITERRA WINERY, SOUTH OF
SANTIAGO, CHILE

THE OWNER AND THE WINEMAKER ARE THE MOST VISIBLE STARS OF THE VINEYARD WORLD. CELEBRATED IN WINE MAGAZINES AND BOOKS, THESE ARE THE PEOPLE WE SEEK OUT WHEN WE WISH TO KNOW MORE ABOUT THE WINES WE PURCHASE AND DRINK. THEIR CUMULATIVE WISDOM AND EXPERIENCES HELP US TO UNDERSTAND THIS BEVERAGE WE SO ENJOY, TO LEARN OF THE HISTORY BEHIND EACH WINE AND WINERY, TO APPRECIATE THE NUANCES OF SMELL AND TASTE, TO NUDGE US TO EXPERIENCE WINE BOTH AS A FINE DRINK IN ITSELF AND AS AN ACCOMPANIMENT TO A MEAL. THE RESPONSIBILITY OF THE SUCCESS OR FAILURE OF THE HARVEST RESTS WITH THESE LEARNED INDIVIDUALS.

FRUITS OF OUR LABOURS

grapes, picking, and people

Yet there is one more individual, often less in the limelight, who should be sharing the honours: the vineyard manager or viticulturalist. Often coming from a family with centuries-old ties to the land, these are the people who nurture the vines to give their best. They are the ones out in all weathers, checking their charges and testing the fruits for ripeness. If, as happens all over the wine-growing world, grapes are being bought in from vineyards other than the winery's own, it is the viticulturalist who ensures that the care these vines are receiving is of sufficient quality.

Along with the vineyard manager is his or her band of vineyard workers, particularly at harvest time, on whose skills the reputation of the winery depends. They, and what nature gives them in the course of a year.

How quick we are to blame the winemaker for the faults of a wine from a vintage which has produced less than exceptional grapes. Unlike its alcoholic siblings, beer and spirits, wine is a drink typically fashioned from a single harvest. This sole-vintage norm has some notable exceptions, including the three kings of the fortified

PREVIOUS PAGE GRAPES ON PARADE AT STAGLIN VINEYARD, A NAPA WINERY RENOWNED FOR ITS CABERNET AND SANGIOVESE

TOP LEFT HARVEST BEGINS AT THE MUMM NAPA WINERY IN MID-AUGUST WITH CHARDONNAY AND PINOT NOIR DESTINED FOR SPARKLING WINE

BELOW LEFT CONDITIONS ALONG THE SAAR RIVER IN GERMANY MEAN THAT LUSCIOUS LATE-HARVEST WINES ARE OFTEN A POSSIBILITY

BELOW CARING FOR YOUR CROP INVOLVES CARING FOR YOUR WORKERS, AS HERE AT A VINEYARD NORTH OF AUCKLAND, IN NEW ZEALAND, WHERE RUBBER GLOVES PROTECT A TONGA ISLANDER'S HANDS DURING HARVEST

world, port, sherry, and madeira, plus Champagne and other sparkling wines. While these wines are also made from one year, for historical and geographical reasons we know them best in their non-vintage forms. That means that the winery has just one chance per year. Get it right, don't muck it up and, by all means, get lucky with the weather. One chance for a year's work to be heralded as magnificent or disparaged as merely ordinary.

The vineyard worker, whether in a group of many or a soul alone, is performing a task that he or she may have been taught by his or her parents who may, in turn, have learned it from a previous generation. The care they exercise reflects their feeling for the place in which they live. They carry with them knowledge essential to the final outcome of the wines we admire.

The nature of the wine world can make the vineyard an international environment. There might be a tradition that those who tend the vines are not the offspring of generations of locals. Instead they may be part of a team from Mexico, Zimbabwe, or Poland, say, perhaps working for the first time in a new land. Or they may be

PREVIOUS PAGE PLUMP AND PERT, HEALTHY CHARDONNAY GRAPES AWAIT THE CRUSH IN ST HELENA, CALIFORNIA

TOP LEFT DESPITE EVERY INNOVATION, PRUNING AND HARVESTING REMAINS HARD ON THE HANDS, MAKING HEAVY-DUTY GLOVES A COMMON SIGHT

BELOW LEFT TURKISH WOMEN ADD AN INTERNATIONAL DIMENSION TO THE HARVEST AT PAUL JABOULET AINE IN THE RHONE VALLEY

ABOVE AS HARVEST-TIME NEARS IN AUSTRALIA, PROTECTION FROM MARAUDING BIRDS BECOMES EVER MORE VITAL

PREVIOUS PAGE LEFT FRESHLY-
PICKED BUCKETS OF PINOT NOIR GRAPES
AT SOUTH AUSTRALIA'S WYNN'S
COONAWARRA ESTATE

PREVIOUS PAGE RIGHT
JABOULET'S SWARTHY TEAM OF
WORKERS ILLUSTRATE HOW MUCH
BACKBREAKING WORK GOES INTO
THE PRODUCTION OF FINE WINE

ABOVE THE OUTDOOR LIFE LEAVES
ITS MARK ON THE FACE OF ONE OF
ANTINORI'S VINEYARD WORKERS IN
THE TUSCAN VILLAGE OF PASSIGNANO

RIGHT EXTREMELY CAREFUL
HARVESTING IS USED IN GERMANY
TO PICK EGON MULLER'S BOTRYTISED
GRAPES FOR HIS SWEET WINES

returning for the twentieth time, carrying with them
knowledge equal to that of the local inhabitants. Either
way, tradition rests with them – for better or for worse.

Tradition in the broadest sense can be either a help or
a hindrance. For example, in Chile the Pais grape (also
known in California as the Mission) was until recently
the most widely-planted varietal because of its high yields
and the ease with which it can be grown. The trouble is
the Pais grape normally makes no better than average-
tasting wine no matter how much care it receives. Yet the
wine fed the local populace, and national pride along
with conservative resistance to change kept Chile wedded
to this lowly grape and unable to enter the world of
fine wine.

This situation didn't really change until the last two
decades of the twentieth century, when Chile's more
outward-looking vintners realized there was a global
demand for wines driven by quality rather than quantity.
Other flavours and textures were wanted, so tradition
gave way to variety, with Cabernet finally overtaking Pais
in the 1990s to head Chile's league of grapes.

PREVIOUS PAGE OLD AND YOUNG
JOIN IN THE HARVEST AT THE POBLET
VINEYARD OF SPAIN'S PIONEERING
MIGUEL TORRES, NEAR BARCELONA

ABOVE IN HOT CLIMATES LIKE THAT
AT NAPA'S ARAUJO VINEYARD, PICKING
IN THE COOL OF THE NIGHT CAN GIVE
GRAPES THE BEST CHANCE OF KEEPING
FRESHNESS AND FRAGRANT AROMAS

RIGHT THE VIBRANT SIGNS OF NEW
GROWTH ON A VINE IN CALIFORNIA'S
NAPA VALLEY

Conversely, what is now "old" will one day be thought of as new. *Provinage* (a method of planting whereby the branch of one vine is bent in an arc and secured in the ground so that the plant will self-propagate) fell out of favour in the early twentieth century because it was deemed to be too chaotic and inefficient. It was replaced by orderly rows of single vines or fields of sensibly-trellised plants. Yet today this more ancient method has found new proponents in areas as diverse as Champagne and Slovenia's Brda region. Too labour-intensive to become popular again, *provinage* is just one of several new "old" developments.

Once planted and of sufficient age to bear wine-worthy grapes, it takes an entire growing season to nurture the fruits of one vintage. Many operations must happen before harvest can occur. Pruning takes place in winter to tidy up a recently-harvested vine and to remove the old growth before the freeze of winter sets in. This can be bitterly cold work or surprisingly warm if the sun chooses to beat down on the vine-covered slope.

Come spring, it's time for "suckering", where the best shoots are selected, and unwanted ones removed. Bug

traps are set and checked and soil moisture readings taken to determine how susceptible the vines might be to moulds. Both of these may force the grower to either spray the vineyard or treat the soils. The all-important training or trellising of the vines takes place at a few stages during the vegetative cycle of spring and summer.

Pruning happens once – or more – in the summer to remove excess growth so that the vine's energy is channelled into the grapes. Any soils lacking essential nutrients must be treated at the right time for the plant to make the best use of any addition. Nitrogenous material in the form of organic or chemical fertilizers is often used, for example. And, in the case of the disease chlorosis, a potassium-based treatment or a choice of roostocks to withstand calcium-rich soils may be added.

Once grapes appear, harvesting is far more involved than merely picking the bunches off the vine. Man meets machine, as grapes are tasted for sweetness and measured for overall ripeness with a refractometer. Only after many careful tests will the vineyard manager be able to decide the optimum time for harvest.

Ripe grapes have many enemies, including heat, sun, and pests. Naturally-occurring bacteria and yeasts living in the air and on the grape skins will attack as readily as wasps, bees, and fruit flies. The effect of any fungal or bacterial infection will be magnified considerably in the warm afternoon sun if the grapes are too tightly clustered together. Humidity doesn't help either. For many, the dark, early mornings, when the balance of sugars and natural acids is at its best, is the time to aim for harvesting.

Once the grapes are deemed perfect, the race is on to remove them from the vine as swiftly as possible so as to take full advantage of both ripeness and aromatic complexity. Weather conditions at harvest are more crucial to the health of the grapes than at any other time in the vineyard cycle. A little light rain can bring refreshment in the hot sun while presenting no danger to the health of the grapes. But if the pickers are too few or too lax, the chances of the crop encountering a serious rainstorm can only increase. Should a deluge arrive, not only can infections spread, but the grapes will

PREVIOUS PAGE CHILE'S EQUABLE CLIMATE MAKES IT A PARADISE FOR THOSE SEEKING TO HARVEST RIPE CHARDONNAY GRAPES

TOP LEFT A HARVEST SUPERVISOR WITH YEARS OF EXPERIENCE IN THE DOURO VALLEY OF PORTUGAL

BELOW LEFT HEARTY FOOD AWAITS VINEYARD AND WINERY WORKERS IN MARTINBOROUGH, NEW ZEALAND

BELOW TIMING THE HARVEST FOR GEWURZTRAMINER IS TRICKY IN ALSACE, AS IT IS EVERYWHERE, TO ENSURE IT DEVELOPS ITS GORGEOUS HEADINESS WITHOUT BECOMING FLABBY

swell with water, diluting the resulting juice. They might even split. What we have is a race against time.

The exception to this is the harvest that takes place late. Whereas table grapes need to look clean and unblemished in order to be saleable, wine grapes need not appear perfect to make fine juice. In fact, some of the best grapes for wine are unappetising to the eye. These grapes are destined for making wines of a richer, typically sweeter style.

There is a multitude of ways that sweet wines can be made, two of the most important being simply to leave the grapes on the vine longer, giving them time to ripen further, or to use grapes affected by noble rot, otherwise known as *botrytis cinerea*. This naturally-occurring mould plays an important role in both Old World and New, being a welcome guest in France, Germany, and Hungary, as well as Canada, Australia, and New Zealand. A gossamer-like mould envelopes the grape, its spores piercing the skin to bring about a range of changes that fundamentally alters the character of the juice. More than half of the grape's water will be lost, making the flavours more concentrated, while the invading fungus transforms

PREVIOUS PAGE THE BIGGER THE TEAM THE QUICKER THE HARVEST, A VITAL FACTOR IN THE VINEYARDS SURROUNDING THE VILLAGE OF MONTCHEVRET IN CHAMPAGNE

TOP LEFT WATER BREAKS IN THE SEARING SUN OF MIGUEL TORRES' VINEYARDS NEAR BARCELONA ARE ESSENTIAL

BELOW LEFT A YOUNG VINE AWAITS ITS TURN FOR PLANTING AT ANTINORI'S WINERY IN ITALY

BELOW DELILLE CELLARS IN WASHINGTON IS RENOWNED FOR THE QUALITY OF ITS AWARD-WINNING BORDEAUX-STYLE REDS

some of the natural sugars and acids into desirably viscous glycerols so sought after by sweet wine fans.

The shallow and sheltered rivers and lakes within Bordeaux's Sauternes, northern France's Anjou-Saumur and Touraine, Hungary's Tokaji, Austria's Burgenland, and Germany's great Riesling districts all conspire to provide a moist climate in the warm autumn days when the grapes are bursting with sugary juice. For noble rot to flourish, this abundant humidity must be matched by a lack of wind, a set of conditions that only occurs in occasional years, making these wondrous wines all the more sought-after. The desire for noble rot doesn't extend to red grapes – this same mould that concentrates the grapes' flavours also destroys their pigmentation.

The weather plays a critical part in one other style of sweet wine: Ice Wine or Eiswein as it is known in Germany and Austria. If grapes can be left undamaged on the vine until winter really sets in, in the early morning hours of a hard frost, the water in the grapes will freeze. Providing the grapes can be picked immediately and transferred to the press room still frozen, the water will

get left behind as ice crystals during pressing, leaving an extremely concentrated juice.

Working in vineyards is always physically demanding, but it can also be entertaining. Pruning and harvesting vines in steep-sloped vineyards like those of port's heartland, the Douro, is far more exciting and demanding. These are the fields that are impossible to mechanise, meaning that everything must be done on foot and by hand. Greater strength is required to stand in vineyards exposed to the elements, but the efforts are repaid with beautiful views of the valley… of the rabbits, deer, and birds that feed and breed among the vines… of the trains, cars, and boats travelling on their way, all the while oblivious to the life and work they pass that surrounds them.

The satisfaction of a job well done, to see the effects of one's labour, is a reward every vineyard worker receives. The pay may be low, but one makes the best of it through enjoyment of a day spent in fine surroundings with one's comrades, sharing nature, life, and the thought that the evening will bring with it a good meal and a glass of last year's crop preserved, as this year's will be… as wine.

PREVIOUS PAGE PORTUGAL'S DOURO VALLEY OFFERS BREATHTAKING VIEWS AS WELL AS BACKBREAKING TOIL

BELOW RED GRAPES LEAD TO RED HANDS DURING HARVEST AT A HUNTER VALLEY WINERY IN AUSTRALIA

RIGHT PLUMP CABERNET GRAPES IN THE NAPA VALLEY BULGING WITH JUICE

LEFT MANY OF THE NEW WORLD'S VINEYARDS ARE PLANTED TO ALLOW MACHINE HARVESTING, AS HERE IN BAROSSA VALLEY, AUSTRALIA

BELOW FIRST STOP AT THE WINERY, THE CRUSHER, SEEN HERE AT PREMIUM PRODUCER, DELILLE CELLARS IN WOODINVILLE, WASHINGTON

THE MOST IMPORTANT PART OF WINEMAKING BEGINS WITH THE SOURCE MATERIAL. IN ORDER TO MAKE GREAT WINE, ONE MUST BEGIN WITH GREAT GRAPES. THE WORK THAT TAKES PLACE IN THE VINEYARD IS FOREMOST IN REGIONS BOTH CLASSICAL AND MODERN. THE HANDLING OF THESE GRAPES ON THEIR WAY TO THE WINERY MUST BE CONTROLLED AND PROTECTED FROM THE FORCES THAT WOULD OTHERWISE TURN A VINTAGE OF SUPERIOR FRUIT INTO ONE THAT IS MERELY GOOD OR EVEN MEDIOCRE. BUT, EVEN IF ALL DUE CARE IS EXERCISED IN THE GROWING, HANDLING, HARVESTING, AND TRANSPORT OF THE RAW MATERIAL, THE NEXT STEP ON ITS JOURNEY IS THE MOST INTENSE AND UNFORGIVING ONE – THE EARLY DAYS SPENT IN THE WINERY.

TOOLS OF THE TRADE

trucks, tools, and tanks

It is generally believed that vines were first domesticated thousands of years ago in the area between the Black Sea and the Caspian Sea in what is now Georgia and Armenia. In those days wine was produced and consumed near where the grapes were grown. Open wooden troughs acted as pressing vessels, and the resulting juice was fermented and stored in clay jars or *amphorae*. These were dug into the ground, leaving a few centimetres peaking out, and proved to be a simple and ingenious storage system, since the wine could be withdrawn as needed until it had run out or spoiled.

It wasn't long before the success of this new drink spread far and wide. The people of the Caucasus ventured southwest to the Mediterranean coast. The Phoenicians of Lebanon and Syria were peaceful, seafaring people who grew wealthy by trading, exchanging wine – and possibly grape vines – with other tribes scattered across the Mediterranean. The first vines are thought to have arrived in France in what is now Marseilles via the ancient Greeks, while the Romans were responsible for introducing viticulture wherever they conquered.

PREVIOUS PAGE FRESHLY-PICKED GRAPES GYRATE THROUGH TO THE CRUSHER AT A NAPA WINERY

BELOW MULTI-AWARD-WINNING STAG'S LEAP WINE CELLARS IN NAPA VALLEY USES GAS HEATERS TO WARD OFF THE RAVAGES OF FROST

RIGHT ROCKFORD WINES IN THE BAROSSA VALLEY SPECIALIZES IN USING TRADITIONAL WINEMAKING EQUIPMENT SUCH AS THIS WELL-WORN BASKET PRESS

Planting a vineyard is some of the most physically taxing work possible. Whether it's bracing a machine for drilling holes in granite in Beaujolais, breaking rocks with a pickaxe in Barossa, or digging by machine in the thick clay-loam of California's Napa Valley, preparing land for young vines drives a lot of dust and dirt into the air. It's both hot and exhausting.

Designing vineyards, especially in the New World, has been taken to amazing lengths. One of the world's largest wineries created a huge, contiguous vineyard in northern California. In doing so, it reshaped the land by creating hills where there were none. The ire of locals was raised, environmentalists were up in arms, but the winery won. When, centuries from now, our descendants look upon this site that may not even continue as a vineyard, will they know that it was created by the hand of humans?

Dogs yelp and truck motors run in the distance. Birds are chirping nearby, flies buzz about, and the crack of a hunter's gun punctuates the relative silence. These are some of the sounds that workers may notice as they pause during their days of building or trellising a new vineyard.

PREVIOUS PAGE FUTURISTIC VISTAS OF STAINLESS STEEL WELCOME VISITORS AT MAJOR COOPERATIVES LIKE THE ONE AT RAUZAN NEAR BORDEAUX

LEFT LIKE A HUGE DRILL BIT, THIS SPIRAL MECHANISM AT WASHINGTON'S CANOE RIDGE ESTATES PROPELS FRESHLY-PICKED GRAPES THROUGH TO THE CRUSHER

ABOVE COPIOUS QUANTITIES OF HOSING ARE FOUND SNAKING AROUND ALL MAJOR WINERIES, LIKE THIS ONE IN THE NAPA VALLEY

It's been said, "wine is art". Art is, among other things, a semblance of shapes and colours. In the vineyard, the three-dimensional geometric interplay between length, width, and depth, is apparent from the start. The choice of laying out a vineyard to take best advantage of the sun, wind, and water, for example, leads to the question of whether the rows should be vertically or horizontally oriented. And, depending on how harvesting is to be done, how far apart should the vines be spaced?

Colour and its many hues vary with the seasons. Brown and grey dominate the colder months, while green, purple, and yellow emerge with the warmer months.

Both the quantity and quality of the grapes of autumn are tied to the white bloom of early spring. Too heavy a shower or too strong a wind might upset the thorough pollination of the flowers, the blossoms that will later become grapes. Fewer grapes later on can mean a higher concentration of flavours, but with that may come a lower yield producing less wine than expected. Sometimes nature will make the decisions for a wine-grower that they might not have chosen for themselves.

PREVIOUS PAGE LEFT SHARP SHEARS LIE POISED FOR THE TASK AHEAD AT YARRA VALLEY WINERY NEAR MELBOURNE

PREVIOUS PAGE RIGHT CLOTHES PEGS IDENTIFY FRUIT FROM DIFFERENT SITES TO HELP AT THE BLENDING STAGE AT COLDSTREAM HILLS, IN VICTORIA

BELOW CLEANING UP AT PRIDE VINEYARD, NAPA VALLEY, INCLUDES REMOVAL OF THE POMACE, THE DEBRIS LEFT AFTER FERMENTATION

BELOW RIGHT FIELDS CAN BE MUDDY AT HARVEST TIME AT POL ROGER IN THE CHAMPAGNE REGION

TOP RIGHT DUMP BINS DEPOSIT THEIR BOOTY AT MARTINBOROUGH, NEW ZEALAND

At different times in the vegetative cycle, the vineyard manager has to decide whether to apply chemical treatments in the form of herbicides, pesticides, or fungicides. Rather than simply relying on chemicals, he or she may choose the more eco-friendly world of organic growing or integrated pest management, whereby bugs are released which are the natural enemies of the pests that prey on either vine or grapes. Alternatively, pheromone-laden traps may be laid to confuse bugs to prevent them reproducing.

Cover crops such as grasses and legumes can be planted between the rows. This serves to discourage or deter the growth of weeds, have competition for water, and nutrients. Spur way grave a compost's biodynamic philosophy. A level is a demanding dogmatic approach to viticulture, with a system whereby phases of the moon govern the timing of specific activities, and involves the application of certain homeopathic preparations at key times during the vineyard cycle.

Whatever courses of action are taken, the appearance of the final fruit need not be as perfect as grapes destined

PREVIOUS PAGE HARVESTED GRAPES
MAKE THE DASH TO THE WINERY AT
CALITERRA, SOUTH OF SANTIAGO, CHILE

ABOVE EVEN AT BORDEAUX WINERIES
LIKE CHATEAU PICHON-LONGUEVILLE,
STEEL TANKS ARE USED FOR
FERMENTING WINE

BELOW RIGHT FLEXIBLE GLOVES
HELP THE SKILLED HARVESTERS IN THE
CARNEROS REGION OF NAPA VALLEY
PICK THE BEST FRUIT

TOP RIGHT A PLASTIC SHOVEL IN
A WAIHEKE ISLAND WINERY, NEAR
AUCKLAND, HANGS READY FOR
POMACE-SHOVELLING DUTIES

for the table simply because wine grapes do not have to rely on their aesthetic properties to be sold in shops.

Alongside the development of an organic movement dedicated to environmental and health objectives, as well as the pursuit of better flavours, the last few decades have seen much effort by wine-growers worldwide to improve the quality of life for their workers, the people who have to live and breathe amongst the vines, by reducing the numbers of times a vineyard has to be sprayed.

Once the vines are producing fruit, when is the best moment to harvest? In an ideal world, harvesting would take place in the cool of night with the vineyard lit up by powerful electric lights, or in the early morning. This is done to maximize the natural acidity within the grapes, a property that can easily plummet in the hot sun. It will also serve to prevent the grape bunches heating up while in transit to the winery, and help to prevent fruit flies and other pests from being attracted to the sweet nectar.

Transporting grapes to cellar in bucket or box requires as much care as any other of the myriad tasks performed throughout the year.

Special attention must be taken in handling thin-skinned varieties such as Pinot Noir and Grenache so as not to damage them. These varieties are rarely harvested by the large machines which scour many modern vineyards, preferring the skilled hands of workers to carefully cut them from the vine.

Generally, white grape varieties tend to ripen sooner than red grapes. Some red grapes are particularly late-ripeners, like the small, thick-skinned Cabernet Sauvignon, and are able to retain their acidity throughout the warm harvest period. The white grape most highly regarded for its ability to keep its complex aromatic profile and brilliant acidity even well into a November harvest is the noble Riesling.

In any wine-producing region, the sight of vineyard workers waiting for a ride at the end of a day – or earlier if it's too hot or too cold – is a common one. If clocking-off time has yet to arrive, the hope will be for a task in the more temperate climate of the cellar. If evening does beckon, it's time to relax and rest in preparation for the next day's labours.

WHETHER ABOVE GROUND OR BELOW, THE CRADLE IN WHICH MANY WINES SLEEP IS THE BARREL. ONCE MERELY A CHEAP AND ACCESSIBLE FORM OF TRANSPORTING VINOUS CARGO, BARRELS FETCH ANYWHERE FROM $250–700 (£120–450), AND ARE PRIZED BY WINE ARTISANS FOR THEIR ABILITY TO PROVIDE GENTLE MATURATION. CCHESTNUT IN ITALY, EUCALYPTUS IN AUSTRALIA, REDWOOD IN CALIFORNIA – THESE WOODS AND OTHERS HAVE ALL BEEN ABANDONED IN FAVOUR OF OAK. TODAY'S BARRELS ARE SOURCED FROM OAK FORESTS SCATTERED ALL OVER THE GLOBE – OREGON, RUSSIA, HUNGARY, GERMANY, AND SLOVENIA AMONGST OTHERS. HOWEVER, NONE ARE SO VALUED FOR THEIR QUALITIES AS THOSE FROM FRANCE AND THE CENTRAL BELT OF THE US.

FROM GRAPE TO WINE

wineries, cellars, barrels, and juice

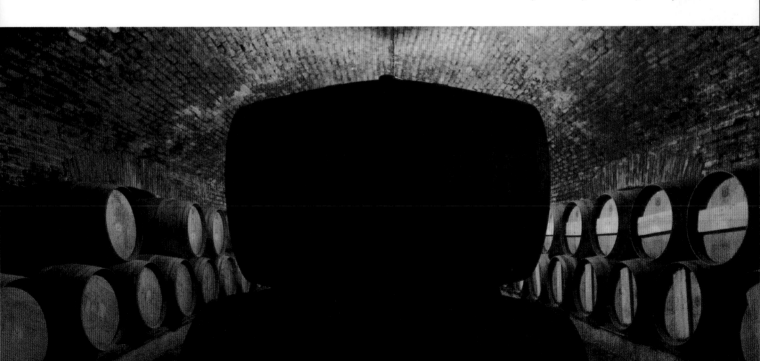

Many see barrels as essential for a wine to mellow, especially reds that begin their lives aggressivley tannic. Before barrels there were clay *amphorae*, but, save a few left in the remote Caucasus mountains of Georgia and a handful of modern iconoclasts, that's ancient history. Other containers available today for maturing wine include those made from cement, stainless steel, and fibreglass.

Specific forests in Europe, especially France, have long been prized for their consistent, fine-grained oak trees. Growing tall and straight, the finest are felled, sawn into manageable sections, and hand-split by coopers. After a number of years spent mellowing in the elements, the wooden planks are chosen by the tightness of their wood grain. Fine-grained wood is more dense, and thus less porous, offering a slower maturation rate. Staves are arranged within circular metal hoops before being "toasted" using a fire of oak chips. The level of toast can greatly affect the final taste as well as being part of the shaping system. The higher the toast, the greater amount of spicy characteristics in the final wine, while a lower toast will let more vanillins leach into the wine.

PREVIOUS PAGE THE IMPOSING ENTRANCE TO CHATEAU MARGAUX, ONE OF THE FIVE BORDEAUX FIRST GROWTHS

ABOVE LEFT THE LEVEL OF TOAST A BARREL RECEIVES WHILE BEING MADE WILL PLAY A ROLE IN THE TASTE OF THE FINAL WINE

BELOW LEFT THE FERMENTATION LOCK ON A BARREL AT LONG VINEYARDS IN NAPA VALLEY

BELOW A STORE OF TREES AT THE ORIGINAL DEMPTOS COOPERAGE IN ST-ROMAIN, BURGUNDY, FROM ONE OF FRANCE'S MOST SOUGHT-AFTER SOURCES, THE VOSGES FOREST IN ALSACE

With barrels so expensive to produce and maintain, many wineries are resorting to the use of oak chips, oak staves inserted into metal tanks, or liquid oak extracts to mimic the effects of ageing a wine in oak barrels. A visit once paid to a French producer yielded a sceptical question from me when I saw several bags of wood chips on his winery floor. His slightly evasive manner when he responded by saying, "Oh, it's for my farm animals' stalls" didn't really allay my suspicions.

But barrels need a place to lie, undisturbed, sometimes for many years, for the maturation magic to take place. Thus what makes a winery isn't only to be found in the design and materials used to fashion its buildings, equally important is the underlying ground. If it was hard rock, it would have been laboriously broken-up with pickaxes or dynamited to yield a home where the precious liquids could rest in a cool, damp nursery.

With the advent of modern refrigeration technology, the task of creating underground cellars has become less significant. Above ground installations require fewer construction costs and take less time to build.

PREVIOUS PAGE LEFT JUST-PRESSED CHARDONNAY JUICE FLOWS FROM A HOME WINEMAKER'S PRESS IN ST HELENA, IN NORTHERN NAPA VALLEY

PREVIOUS PAGE RIGHT THE REGALIA OF BURGUNDY'S CONFRERIE DES CHEVALIERS DU TASTEVIN, ONE OF WINE'S MOST VENERATED BROTHERHOODS

LEFT A CLOTH PROVIDES A STRONG SEAL FOR THE BUNG AT ROCKFORD WINES, BAROSSA VALLEY, AUSTRALIA

ABOVE THE ICONIC TOWER OF BORDEAUX'S FAMOUS CHATEAU LATOUR DOUBLES UP AS A DOVECOTE

Clos et Domaine
d'Ardhuy
Clos des Langres

For many businesses these days, exterior aesthetics have become as important as the technical aspects of the interior. One of the most impressive new "old" wine technology experiences I have seen was when leading viticulturalist Tim Mondavi showed me round the family firm's flagship Oakville winery in Napa Valley. Completed at a cost of $27 million (£14.3 million), fifty-six French open-top oak vats, each with a 227 hectolitre capacity, stand upright on the second level of a new 1,858 square-metre (20,000 square-feet) fermentation room. The bottom level of the building houses an equally large underground cellar holding 1,300 barriques of 225 litres each. No need for pumps here, the "new" wines from the upper tier flow down into the smaller barrels in the lower tier to rest until they are ready for blending.

Winemakers eager for other new "old" methods to improve their wines are even experimenting with designs based on Feng Shui principles.

Another breathtaking example of the New World marrying successfully with the Old is in Castello Banfi's large facility in the picturesque Montalcino region of

PREVIOUS PAGE LEFT STERLING VINEYARDS' BELL TOWER IN NAPA VALLEY BY THE LIGHT OF THE MOON

PREVIOUS PAGE RIGHT THE CHAPEL CEILING AT THE SANTA RITA WINERY IN CHILE'S MAIPO VALLEY

ABOVE FRESHLY-FILTERED PORT POURS INTO A CONTAINER AT DOW'S BOMFIM WINERY IN PORTUGAL'S DOURO VALLEY REGION

BELOW RIGHT CRUSHING GRAPES THE TRADITIONAL WAY AT HOME IN ST HELENA, NAPA VALLEY

TOP RIGHT FRESHLY PRESSED WINE AT AUSTRALIAN WINERY, ROCKFORD

southern Tuscany. The approach to the American-owned castle/winery – the landscaping and the vineyards – and the design and technology that filled the cellar put me in mind of my native California. "Napa comes to Tuscany", was my first thought – a feeling shared by many Italian traditionalists when the estate was first built. The end results – what's in the glass – are what finally matters, and eventually the sniping ended. In subsequent years the owners, the Mariani family of New York, even inspired a few imitators, albeit on a less grand scale.

Levels of evaporation in cellars are of great concern to anyone involved in the making of wine or spirits. Thus cellars are often deliberately built near bodies of water to increase the humidity of the ambient air, thereby slowing the rate of evaporation from the wine in the barrel. Some cellar managers have installed advanced humidification systems, while others have introduced continuously flowing water in an attempt to draw nature's forces into balance. A far simpler method is to spray water on an earthen or sandy floor. Though more labour-intensive, this slows evaporation quite considerably.

Interestingly, with sweet wines less water is lost through evaporation than alcohol. The density of sugary wines "pushes" the alcohol through the grains of the wooden barrels at a faster rate than in dry wines. This is most apparent in the Jerez region of southern Spain, where sherry producers have often remarked upon the concentration of alcohol in old barrels of their drier amontillados and olorosos, and the diminishing of it in their luscious, raisiny Pedro Ximénez wines.

So once in the cellar, what next? All of the things a grape needs to transform itself into wine are already present within and atop the grape: water, acidity, proteins, enzymes, yeasts, and sugars. Most wineries these days add wine yeasts to ensure a predictable fermentation, and some will add enzymes to ensure the yeasts do their jobs properly. Tannins are occasionally added to give a wine any structure it might lack, while acidity can be used to correct a wine in an unusually hot vintage, or to give "backbone" to wines from grapes grown in a particularly warm climate. Use of too much added acidity can be easily spotted by the trained palate.

Sugar is often added to wines, even some of the world's finest, to boost not sweetness, but alcohol. This process is called chaptalization, after the French chemist who invented it, Jean-Antoine Chaptal. This not only increases the wine's alcoholic strength, but also broadens its texture and mouthfeel. With improved growing techniques and global warming, the need for chaptalization has lessened in recent years.

All that is needed now is for the grapes to release and combine these elements. The wooden and stone presses of yesterday have given way to today's pneumatic and vacuum presses. The original methods did a good job of extracting the juice but, if the winemaker wasn't extremely careful, they also managed to extract unpleasant, green-tasting tannins from the grape pips.

One venerable approach barely in use is the human foot. Often simply put on as a show for wine tourists, the exhausting and time-consuming task of foot treading is still carried out for the finest ports, and in a few other places in the world. During a visit to leading port estate Quinta do Vesuvio at the end of harvest, I compared three

samples made from different pressings: one done by foot, one by the winery's own automatic machine, and one from a pneumatic press. My host, Rupert Symington, felt that there was little difference between the three, but my palate told me otherwise. For me, the wines extracted by foot possessed finer, softer tannins of a quality just above those of the wines from the new machine which were, in turn, better than those from the pneumatic press.

Fermentation is simply the action of yeasts and enzymes transforming sugars into carbon dioxide, heat, and alcohol. The yeasts and enzymes slow or stop working when either all the sugars have been used, or the alcohol level becomes high enough to weaken or halt the yeast's activity, or when sulphur dioxide is added to finish the process. The gurgle of the fermenting juice stored in barrels and tanks punctuates the air, creating soft ripples of sound echoing throughout the cellar.

Other sounds commonly found in wineries of a less romantic nature are the humming and whirring of machines. Pumps help to move wine from one vessel to another, filtering devices provide the comfort of a stable

wine to a vintner whose year's efforts can be destroyed with improper handling.

The fermented wine, when placed in barrel, will be hazy or cloudy. Though filtering is used by some wineries to produce a stable product, the gentlest way of removing suspended matter is over time, through a series of "rackings". After a number of rackings, the wine from all barrels chosen for a particular bottling will be placed into a large stainless-steel tank for its final blending, or "marriage". After weeks or months spent in blending vats, the settled wines are fined and/or filtered before the final steps are taken to bring the wine to the table.

Workers in the wineries and cellars – the "cellar rats" – need an even greater commitment and enthusiasm to the vision of great wine than those employed in the vineyards. Nature provides ready inspiration for those in the fields, while the damp and temperate ambience and the quiet of the cellars can be monotonous for many. Although cellars can be slow places to work, one of the advantages is the opportunity – practically compulsory, even – to sample wines in all stages of their evolution.

PREVIOUS PAGE LOCAL FOREST FIRES COLOUR THE SUNRISE AT TURNBULL WINERY IN NAPA VALLEY, HIGHLIGHTING LOCAL ARCHITECTURE ORIGINALLY INSPIRED BY THE EARLY RUSSIAN SETTLEMENT OF FORT ROSS

LEFT A PRIVATE PARTY DINES IN THE ATMOSPHERIC CELLAR OF MARKHAM WINERY IN ST HELENA, CALIFORNIA

BELOW AS SEEN HERE WITH CHARDONNAY JUICE IN THE VILLAGE OF VERGISSON, BURGUNDY, THE TIME-CONSUMING YET VITAL TASK OF RACKING SEPARATES MATURING WINE FROM ITS SEDIMENT

PRECEDING THE ADVENT OF GLASS BOTTLES WITH CORK STOPPERS, WINES WERE TRANSPORTED FROM WINERY TO HOSTELRY OR HOME IN A WOODEN BARREL SEALED WITH A REMOVABLE WOODEN BUNG. WINES WOULD BE DRAWN OFF BY THE INN OR SHOPKEEPER WITH A SPIGOT INTO WAITING BUCKETS, MUGS, CUPS, OR PREFERABLY GLASSES BEFORE PASSING THE LIPS OF THE DRINKER. THIS WAS A REASONABLE WAY TO GET WINE FROM MAKER TO CONSUMER WHEN MOST DRINKING TOOK PLACE IN INNS AND PUBLIC HOUSES. CENTRAL HEATING AND TELEVISION HAD YET TO BE INVENTED, SO PEOPLE WERE MORE THAN READY TO GATHER IN THESE WARM AND COMMUNAL PLACES TO DRINK AND SOCIALIZE WITH THEIR COLLEAGUES, FRIENDS, NEIGHBOURS, AND EVEN STRANGERS.

THE NEW VINTAGE

bottles, corks, and tasting

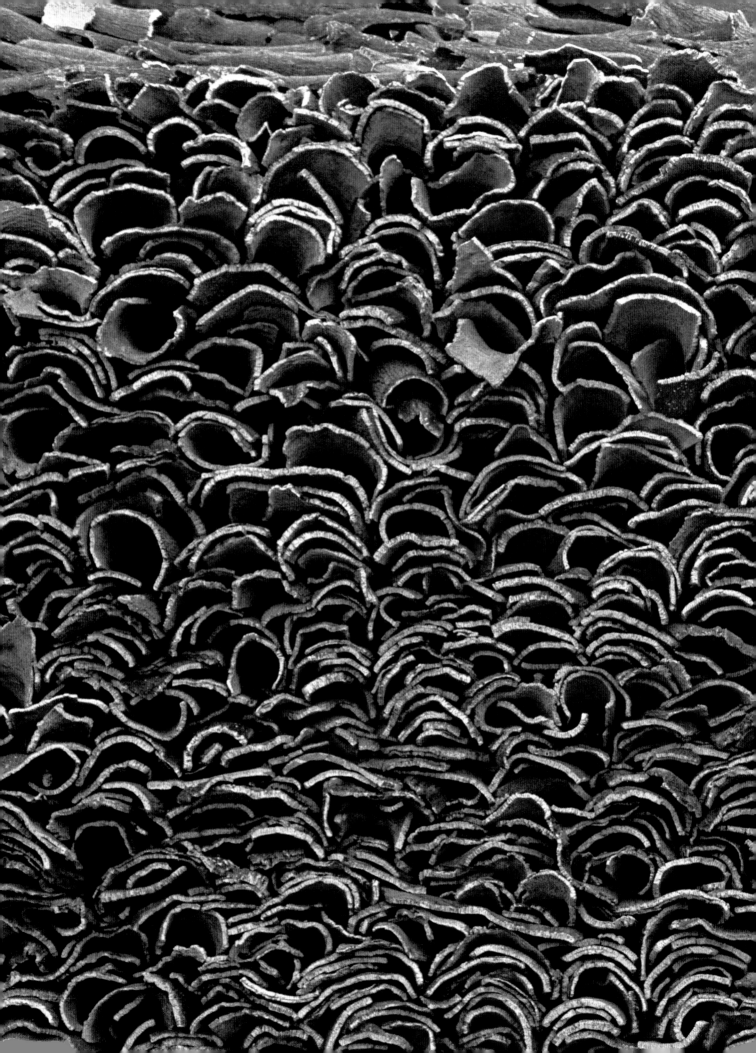

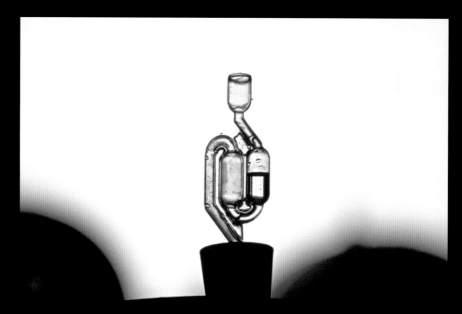

Over the years, bottle shapes have evolved from wider, stumpier versions to the narrow forms we know today. Labels, now vital as carriers of legally-required information as well as a way of distinguishing one wine from another, were preceded by simple whitewashed markings indicating a wine's vintage and producer, and nothing more. The most significant occurrence in bottle fabrication was probably the development of bottles strong enough to withstand the intense pressures of the world's favourite sparkling wine, Champagne.

Certain bottle shapes are inextricably linked to the wines of a particular region. Alsace has its graceful tapering *flĕtes*, Baden and Franken their colourfully-named *bocksbeutels,* while Chianti will long be remembered for its wicker-encased *fiaschi.*

Without question, the bottling process is the least romantic part of winemaking. Very few words have been spared to describe this tedious but essential process of winemaking to the layperson. I will now set about disturbing this tradition – but only slightly. If approached as one does necessary household chores such as washing the dishes, as a form of meditation working on bottling

PREVIOUS PAGE INSPECTING THE CORK BARK AT THE AMORIM & IRMAOS PLANT IN PORTUGAL. THE BARK IS BOILED, DRIED, AND STAMPED TO FORM TWO MILLION CORK CLOSURES A DAY

ABOVE LEFT THE CALM OF THE CELLAR AT THE HISTORIC MULLER-SCHARZHOF WINERY IN THE SAAR PROVIDES PERFECT CONDITIONS FOR ITS CLASSIC RIESLINGS

BELOW LEFT THE SIGHT OF CARBON DIOXIDE BUBBLING THROUGH A FERMENTATION LOCK AT NEW ZEALAND'S CLOUDY BAY WINERY INDICATES ACTIVITY

BELOW BOTTLING LINES SUCH AS THIS AT COLUMBIA CREST WINERY IN WASHINGTON, PRODUCE THOUSANDS OF BOTTLES A DAY

lines isn't so bad. With thoughts of life's larger questions drifting through your mind and music playing on a nearby radio, the time passes more quickly than one might expect. The clatter of the bottles bumping into one another is occasionally punctuated by the sound of breaking glass when one of these soldiers breaks rank, crashing into its brothers and causing a pause in the din as the line is shut down and the errant bottle extricated from the machine's clutches.

As well as the means of transport, our vessel must protect the newly-bottled wine. In order to eliminate unwanted oxygen, a heavier-than-air inert gas can be injected or sprayed into the empty bottle before filling. Another preservation method is to add a dose of sulphur dioxide, an antioxidant, to the bottle after filling. Either way, a stopper must be swiftly driven in or fixed on top of the bottle to ensure these gases do not escape. Traditionally, these closures have been fashioned from cork.

The forests of Portugal and, to a lesser degree, Spain are homes of a unique species of oak, the *Quercus suber*. Of Mediterranean origin, it grows primarily in hilly, open

PREVIOUS PAGE LEFT YOUNG WINE IS INSPECTED AT VARIOUS STAGES OF ITS MATURATION, AS HERE AT THE ST CLEMENT WINERY IN ST HELENA

PREVIOUS PAGE RIGHT THE REGIMENTED UNIFORMITY OF THE BOTTLING LINE AT MIGUEL TORRES WINERY, NEAR BARCELONA

ABOVE LEFT CORK HARVESTER JOAQUINA MARIA LUCAS ARSENIO TRIMS BITS OF CORK FROM BRANCHES OF DEAD OAKS, WITH AN UMBRELLA PROVIDING SHADE FROM THE FIERCE SUN. THE BARK WILL BE USED TO MAKE CORK GRANULES, A SPECIALTY OF THE VILLAGE OF SANTANA DO MATO, PORTUGAL

BELOW LEFT POISED TO TAKE A SAMPLE, THE "WINE THIEF" AND A GLASS ON BARRELS AT PETER LEHMANN WINES IN AUSTRALIA'S BAROSSA VALLEY

ABOVE DEMONSTRATION OF FINISHED CORK AT A MUSEUM IN PORTUGAL

woodlands, and slopes. It is estimated that the sixty square-kilometres (twenty-three square-miles) of Portugal's cork forests provide it with its main agricultural export, ironically surpassing even its wines. Once they reach twenty-five, cork trees can be harvested every ninth year. With its thick bark, the outer layer can be stripped without fear of the tree being damaged while the new layer grows.

Cork's unique selling point is its small, closely-packed micro-structure of cells which makes it both an elastic seal and – theoretically – inert. Unfortunately, moulds that naturally exist in bark sometimes manage to survive processing and sterilization, and end up affecting the wine the cork is supposed to be protecting. Cork taint can be recognized by its musty or cardboard-like aroma, and transmits a taste that seems to "flatten out" the wine, stripping it of its fruit. Industry estimates suggest that the number of cork-tainted bottles lies between three and ten per cent. While the cork industry strives to reduce these problems, cork is still the preference of most producers. Other closures are on the increase and do receive more attention, but cork is still by far the leading stopper.

PREVIOUS PAGE SAMPLES FROM VATS OF NEWLY-FERMENTED SPARKLING WINES AWAIT ANALYSIS IN THE LABORATORY AT THE MUMM NAPA WINERY IN CALIFORNIA

BELOW THE FIRST NECESSITY IN ANY BOTTLING LINE LIKE THIS ONE AT VINA AQUITANIA, CHILE, IS CLEAN BOTTLES

RIGHT BOTTLES MARCH TOWARDS THE LABELLING MACHINE AT THE STELLENBOSCH FARMERS WINERY

So what is the role of humans in the final wine? According to Paul Draper of California's Ridge Vineyard, "Even in California, every wine is a terroir wine. The question is, is it a poor, mediocre, good, or great terroir wine? One of my favourite California wines is from a blend of five vineyards, though one could make the argument that by blending it, the terroir is less succinctly expressed than that same winery's single vineyard bottling. The deciding factor in whether or not wine expresses 'place' is the degree of human intervention in the wine. Terroir is meaningless unless there exists a wine-grower with a vision of the highest potential of what a particular piece or pieces of land can bring. Knowledge, experience, and financing all factor into this equation."

A willingness not to sacrifice one's vision to market or ownership forces is an additional attribute essential to achieving this goal. Thus wines may provide us with a sense of place. "The war for terroirism is proceeding fine," says Draper's fellow Santa Cruzan, winery owner Randall Grahm. "As it disappears, it's appreciated more – like a species creeping towards extinction."

PREVIOUS PAGE DEEP UNDER THE STREETS OF EPERNAY, FRANCE, A CELLAR WORKER INSPECTS THE MATURING CHAMPAGNE AT POL ROGER

ABOVE LEFT HANDS OF MAX LONGIS, CELLARMASTER AT THE SALON CHAMPAGNE HOUSE, WHOSE WINES ARE MADE SOLELY FROM CHARDONNAY

BELOW LEFT CUSTOMERS AT THE L'INTENDANT WINE SHOP IN BORDEAUX ARE SPOILT FOR CHOICE WITH THE WINES FROM 160 LOCAL CHATEAUX STORED AROUND A SPIRALLING RAMP

BELOW NOT ALL WINE SHOPS ARE SO MODERN, BUT ALL PRIDE THEMSELVES ON THE QUALITY OF THEIR PRODUCE

Location can affect the sensory impression of a wine, too. The most unusual example of this for me took place when I visited the Hochar family at its winery in Lebanon. Joined by a few wine tourists, I was guided through the cellars by patriarch Serge and his son Gaston. Among the many wines we tasted was a vintage from the early 1970s. Opened on the lowest level of the cellar, we savoured this rarity over several minutes. Serge asked us to walk up the stairs to the next level before suggesting we tried the wine once more. We found that the wine's aroma and flavour had altered. Had the wine changed so quickly over so little time? Probably not, it had only been a minute. Was it the change in elevation? Unlikely. Was it due to a change of ambient light, humidity, or smells? Possibly, but none that we noticed. The final demonstration took place upon our emergence from the cellars into the shaded terrace and the waiting sunlight above. The variables here were clear – light, sound, smell. Save our companions, all had changed. Then again, so had the wine. A slightly bemused, beatific smile accompanied by a subtle shoulder shrug was all that Serge proffered by way of explanation.

Visiting a wine-growing and winemaking location, being informed about it by someone knowledgeable, seeing the place where a wine is made, and finally tasting that wine in that special site imprints both the conscious and subconscious parts of the mind with sensory memories that cannot be duplicated in a classroom or home setting. Tasting that wine again will elicit memories that will return one to that eloquent initial location.

When the wine is ready, and someone ready for the wine, there must be someone willing to open the bottle and pour the wine. In a restaurant, the sommelier is the professional called upon to perform this task. He or she has undergone rigorous training in keeping a cellar in proper working order, in the care of the wine and its vessels, and has tasted many wines in order to assess a wine's correctness and its suitability for an occasion. While not as physically taxing a job as digging holes for new vines, nor as intricate as, say, accounting for the year's receipts, being a "somm" is no easy task. It is, however, certainly one of the most enjoyable that I can think of.

PREVIOUS PAGE TASTING SAMPLES OF THE LATEST VINTAGE OF CHATEAU PICHON-LONGUEVILLE, ONE OF BORDEAUX'S TOP CLASSIFIED GROWTHS

LEFT BUNDLED CORK BARK AT SAO PAIO DE OLEIROS. THESE SMALL PIECES WILL BE USED TO MAKE GRANULATED BOTTLE STOPPERS AND CORK FLOORING

BELOW CORKS AT THE CHAMPCORK FACTORY AT SANTA MARIA DE LAMAS, PORTUGAL, DESTINED TO BE BOTTLE STOPPERS FOR SPARKLING WINES

Where are we placed when tasting wine? A damp winery cellar will provide an experience intrinsically different to that of your home cellar or your dining table. Wherever, this is an experience to savour. The nuance of the wine's colour changes with time as it begins to oxidize in the presence of air. While white wines take on a more golden shade, reds venture towards the rust and coppery hues of the spectrum. As a wine ages, the initial excitement of primary aromas of fruits and flowers evolve into an enticing subtle, tertiary bouquet of earth and herbs. With time in bottle, the fruit and oak that capture both critic and consumer become intertwined, diminishing the potentially overpowering strength of each one while growing into something delightfully separate and altogether special, like two individuals who've known each other for many years.

Remember that the enjoyment of wine is for all of your senses, and for your imagination, too. Wherever you might be, the opportunity to understand its historical and cultural references, the work that goes into making it, and the place from which it originates will enrich the moment.

PREVIOUS PAGE IN THE 1980S THE OWNERS OF CALIFORNIA'S BERINGER VINEYARDS FOUND THIS SECRET STASH OF WINES HIDDEN DURING PROHIBITION

BELOW A WINEMAKER AT VINA AQUITANIA NEAR SANTIAGO SQUEEZES A CABERNET SAUVIGNON GRAPE TO TEST WHETHER IT IS "LA PINTA". BEING ABLE TO SQUEEZE JUICE FROM THE GRAPE IS A SIGN IT IS READY TO HARVEST

RIGHT THERE CAN BE NO BETTER WAY TO SAMPLE WINES THAN IN A TUTORED TASTING, AS HERE IN RUDD WINERY'S UNDERGROUND CELLARS IN NAPA

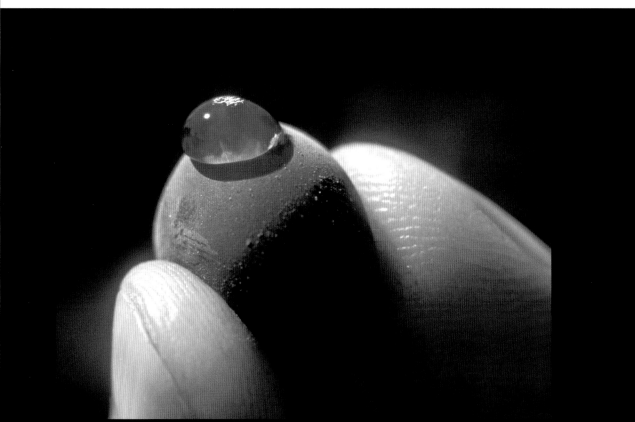

ACKNOWLEDGMENTS

FROM CHARLES

The photographs for this book, especially with its worldwide coverage, could not have happened without the help of many individuals. Hilary Lumsden and Mitchell Beazley believed in and supported the concept and publication of this book. David Furer came to the book with a fresh view of the wine industry and all its people and places.

From Corbis I got great support from Sid Hastings, Charles Mauzy, Win Scudder, Peter Howe and Carl Gronquist. My close friend Patrick Cronenberger of Bordeaux was my expert translator for many months in Europe. Robert and Margrit Mondavi generously provided introductions to their many friends around the world, while my wife Daphne gave me limitless support. National Geographic editors, Bill Garrett and Bob Gilka, dispatched me into wine country nearly 30 years ago for my first professional look at this industry. Assistance with the concept for the book came from Jennifer Barry while Janice Fuhrman brought her valuable wine knowledge to the initial dummy for the book. And, certainly, my mother Ada O'Rear who inspired me with her ideas, energies, and encouragement from the day my two feet hit the planet.

FROM DAVID

Thanks to my parents Howard Furer and Roberta Corwin whose unending love and encouragement have provided me with the foundation to get this far. Extra applause to Howie for keeping the cellar and many other things!

To Helmut Doka without whose generous and loyal friendship, inquiring mind, and big ears I may not have discovered the joys and knowledge of this favorite of beverages and to his patient wife Frauke for putting up with us. Denise Young whose strength and humor always impress. Peter Werbe for helping me to "keep it real" over the years by reminding me that not everyone who likes wine is as lucky as I to taste the greats. Gail Lockwood for looking out for my heart for so many years – I still mourn the bottle of wine behind your sofa! Robert Rohden who taught me much about the wine trade and kept me laughing when times were tough. Hilary for the faith and Susanna for the tweaking.

Finally, I want to express gratitude to all the wineries who have accommodated my visits, inquiries, and consumption these past fourteen years – you're a patient bunch whom I hope to have honored on these pages.